HOW TO NOT be THAT Camper

How to NOT BE THAT CAMPER

Campground Etiquette for
People Who Mean Well

ERIN GRAVES

DEDICATION

To the campground neighbors who helped shape my understanding of etiquette,
whether you meant to or not.

And to the people I camped next to in my twenties…
please accept this book as my formal apology.

INTRO

A QUICK NOTE BEFORE YOU SET UP CAMP

Camping is one of those things that sounds simple, until you're actually doing it next to other people.

Other people with different schedules. Different noise tolerances. Different ideas of how bright lights should be, how early is "too early," and whether dog poop counts as "someone else's problem."

Most of us don't set out to be *that* camper. We're just trying to relax, make memories, and enjoy our time outside. But campgrounds are shared spaces, and sometimes the things that feel normal, or harmless, to us are exactly the things driving someone else quietly insane three sites over.

This book isn't about rules for the sake of rules. It's not about camping the "right" way or telling anyone how to have fun. And it's definitely not about shaming anyone who's ever accidentally annoyed a neighbor. (If that were the case, none of us would be safe.)

This book is about awareness.
About those little things that make a big difference.
About how a few small adjustments can turn a good camping trip into a great one, for you *and* the people around you.

You don't need a fancy rig.
You don't need years of experience.
You just need to remember that you're not camping alone.

Before we dive in, let's start with a quick, just-for-fun quiz. No judgment. No scoring. Just a moment of self-reflection that may or may not make you laugh uncomfortably.

Ready?

ARE YOU THE PROBLEM?

A QUICK CAMPGROUND SELF-CHECK

Before we talk about campground etiquette, let's do a little self-reflection.
Not the deep, emotional kind. The campground kind.

1 It's 10:30pm at the campground. Your site is still lively. You think:

A. "Time to take this inside."
B. "We'll wrap it up soon."
C. "One more story won't hurt."
D. "Quiet hours are a suggestion."

2 Your dog wanders toward another campsite. You:

A. Call them back immediately.
B. Follow closely, just in case.
C. Assume it's fine. They're friendly.
D. Realize you don't have a poop bag.

3 Your campsite lighting after dark looks like:

A. Soft, minimal, and cozy.
B. On when needed, off when not.
C. Decorative and very visible.
D. An airport runway

4 There's a tempting shortcut through someone's campsite. You:

A. Pretend you never saw it.
B. Consider it, then keep walking.
C. Hug the edge and move quickly.
D. Commit fully and walk through like you belong there.

5 Departure morning for you usually sounds like:

A. Quiet, calm, and low-key.
B. A little movement, but respectful.
C. Doors opening and closing... a lot.
D. Preparations for a demolition.

6 You realize something you're doing might be affecting your neighbors. Your first instinct is:

A. Adjust immediately.
B. Check in and be more aware.
C. Hope no one says anything.
D. Assume it's probably fine.

IF YOU CHOSE:

Mostly A's
You're the camper people hope parks next to them.

Mostly B's
You're doing great. A little awareness goes a long way.

Mostly C's
You may be flirting with THAT camper territory, but you're still very likable.

Mostly C's
This book is about to be extremely helpful for you. Welcome.

CHAPTER ONE

NOISE:

THE FASTEST WAY TO MAKE ENEMIES AT A CAMPGROUND

There are a lot of ways to ruin a perfectly good camping trip. Bad weather. Forgetting the coffee. Realizing you left the leveling blocks at home.

But nothing, NOTHING, creates campground tension faster than noise.

Noise travels differently at a campground. It doesn't matter how far apart sites look on the map. Sound carries. Conversations echo. Music floats. And that generator you swear is "not that loud" suddenly feels like it's parked directly inside someone else's bedroom.

If you want a peaceful camping experience, understanding campground noise etiquette isn't optional. It's essential.

How to Accidentally become THAT camper

Let's say quiet hours start at 10pm.

At 9:59pm, you turn up the music just a little because technically, it's still allowed. At 10:07pm, you're deep into a story that absolutely cannot wait until morning. Someone laughs loudly. A chair scrapes across gravel. A cooler lid slams shut like it's mad at the world.

Meanwhile, your neighbor is lying in bed, staring at the ceiling, wondering if this is how campground feuds begin.

Noise doesn't have to be excessive to be annoying. Repetitive sounds, sudden bursts of laughter, and ongoing conversations are often worse than one loud moment. And late at night, even "normal" noise feels amplified.

Why This Actually Matters

People go camping to rest. Some have been driving all day. Some are waking up early. Some are camping with kids who finally fell asleep after an hour-long bedtime negotiation.

When noise spills over into someone else's site, it takes away their ability to relax in their own space. That's when frustration starts building. And once that happens, everything else feels more irritating than it should.

Campgrounds are shared environments. Quiet hours aren't about being strict or joyless. They exist so everyone gets a fair shot at enjoying their stay.

What to Do Instead

You don't have to whisper or sit in silence like you're in timeout. A few simple habits go a long way.

- Start winding things down before quiet hours begin
- Lower music gradually instead of cutting it abruptly
- Move late-night conversations inside your RV
- Be mindful of doors, storage compartments, and chairs after dark
- If you wouldn't want to hear it from someone else's site, it's probably too loud
- During the day, keep music at a level that stays within your own campsite. If it's clearly audible several sites away, it's too much. Even if it's a great playlist.

Generators: A Special Kind of Noise

Generators deserve their own moment.

They are useful. They are sometimes necessary. They are also the fastest way to become that camper if used without consideration.

If your campground allows generators, follow the posted hours exactly. Running one early in the morning or late at night is a guaranteed way to upset everyone around you.

If you rely on a generator:

- Use it during approved hours only
- Keep it as far from neighboring sites as possible

- Turn it off as soon as you're done

Just because a generator is allowed doesn't mean it's appreciated at all times.

CAMPGROUND KARMA

The thing about noise is that it comes back around.

The camper you keep awake tonight might be the one packing up at dawn tomorrow. The group you annoyed with music might be the same group chatting loudly while you're trying to nap.

Campground karma has excellent timing.

Being mindful of noise isn't about being perfect. It's about being aware that other people are sharing the same space, and the same thin layer of patience.

ASK YOURSELF THIS

- Would I be annoyed if this sound were coming from the site next to me?
- Is this noise necessary right now?
- Could this wait until morning?

If the answer makes you hesitate... adjust accordingly.

Bottom Line

You can still laugh, talk, and enjoy your camping trip without becoming the unofficial entertainment for the entire campground.

A little awareness goes a long way. It will make your trip, and everyone else's, a whole lot better.

CHAPTER TWO

SPACE AND BOUNDARIES:

JUST BECAUSE YOU CAN WALK THERE, DOESN'T MEAN YOU SHOULD

Campgrounds give the illusion of extra space. Wide roads. Open grassy areas. Picnic tables scattered like invitations.

But make no mistake, every campsite is someone's temporary home. And nothing breaks campground peace faster than someone forgetting where *their* space ends and *someone else's* begins.

Boundaries matter. Not in a dramatic way. In a "please don't step over my sewer hose" kind of way.

How to Accidentally become THAT camper

You're heading to the bathhouse, the playground, or your friend's site across the loop. Instead of taking the road, you cut straight through another campsite.

It's just a shortcut. No big deal.

Except you walk between their chairs. You enter their dog's territory, that may or may not appreciate new visitors. You step over a power cord. You pass close enough that they pause their conversation and track your movement like they're watching wildlife.

Now imagine this happens again. And again. And again.

Congratulations! You've officially become *that* camper.

Campers don't love surprise foot traffic through their living room. And yes, that's what their campsite is: their living room, kitchen, and front porch all rolled into one.

WHY THIS ACTUALLY MATTERS

Campsites are designed with intentional boundaries, even if they aren't marked with fences. When someone cuts through a site, it disrupts privacy and comfort.

It also creates safety issues:

- Tripping hazards from cords and hoses
- Kids and pets being startled
- Equipment getting damaged

Most campers don't want confrontation. They'll smile politely while quietly hoping you choose literally *any other path* next time.

What to Do Instead

The fix here is simple—and it applies to almost everything campground-related.

- Stick to roads and designated paths
- Assume every campsite is occupied, even if no one is outside
- Walk *around*, not through
- Treat cords, hoses, and mats like invisible walls

If you wouldn't walk through someone's hotel room to get to the ice machine, don't do it at a campground.

Slide-Outs, Awnings, and the "Shared Space" Illusion

Slide-outs and awnings are great. They give you room to spread out and relax.

But they also don't magically turn shared space into private property.

Be mindful of:

- How far your awning extends
- Where your chairs end up
- Whether your setup blocks foot traffic or access points

If someone has to awkwardly shuffle sideways to pass your site, things may have gone too far.

Kids, Dogs, and Boundary Blur

Campgrounds are fun. Kids explore. Dogs sniff. That's normal.

What's not normal is letting kids or pets regularly wander into other campsites without permission. Friendly doesn't mean invited.

A good rule of thumb:

- If it's not your site, ask first.
- If no one's outside, it's a no.
- If you wouldn't want it happening to you, rein it in.

Most campers are happy to be friendly—once introductions happen. Surprise visits? Not so much.

Campground Karma

Today, you cut through someone else's campsite. Tomorrow, someone walks right through yours…while you're eating dinner.

Campground karma doesn't rush, but it *never* misses.

Respecting boundaries keeps the peace and makes the campground feel more relaxed for everyone. Including you.

Ask Yourself This

- Would this feel intrusive if it were happening at my site?

- Am I treating this space like a shortcut or someone's home?
- Is there an easy alternative path? There almost always is.

Bottom Line

Campgrounds work best when everyone stays in their lane. Literally.

Respecting space and boundaries isn't about being unfriendly. It's about letting everyone enjoy their temporary home without feeling crowded, watched, or tiptoed through.

CHAPTER THREE

PETS & KIDS:
WHEN "THEY'RE JUST BEING FRIENDLY" ISN'T ENOUGH

Campgrounds are full of life. Kids riding bikes. Dogs sniffing every possible blade of grass. Laughter echoing down the loop.

All of that is part of the charm...until it spills into someone else's campsite without an invitation.

Pets and kids are welcome at campgrounds. Surprise campsite visits, however, are not.

How to Accidentally become THAT camper

Your dog wanders over to a neighboring campsite. You smile and say, "Don't worry, they're friendly!"

Meanwhile, your neighbor is wondering:

- If your dog is actually friendly.
- If it's going to hurt their pets, or vice-versa.
- If they're now responsible for someone else's pet.

Nearby, kids zip through campsites on bikes, cutting between chairs and fire rings. Someone's nap is interrupted. A conversation stops mid-sentence. A chair gets knocked over.

You assume everyone understands. "This is camping."

Not everyone does.

WHY THIS ACTUALLY MATTERS

Not all campers love dogs. Not all campers are comfortable around kids they don't know. And some campers are dealing with:

- Allergies
- Anxiety around animals
- Sleeping babies
- Reactive pets
- Limited patience after a long travel day

When pets or kids wander into other campsites, it removes someone's ability to relax in their own space. Even well-behaved pets and polite kids can cause stress when boundaries aren't clear.

What to Do Instead

Good campground etiquette doesn't mean keeping everyone silent or contained. It just means being present and aware.

For pets:

- Keep dogs leashed unless in designated areas.
- Walk them *around* campsites, not through them.
- Pick up after them immediately.
- Don't assume friendliness equals welcome.

For kids:

- Set clear boundaries about where they can play.
- Encourage using roads, paths, and common areas.
- Remind them that campsites are private spaces.
- Keep an eye on volume, especially early and late.

Teaching kids campground etiquette is part of the camping experience, and it benefits everyone.

Bikes, Scooters, and Speed

Campgrounds feel safe, which makes it easy to forget that vehicles, pets, and pedestrians all share the same space.

- Keep speeds slow.
- Watch for younger kids.
- Be extra mindful around blind corners.

A peaceful campground stays peaceful when everyone looks out for one another.

CAMPGROUND KARMA

Today, your dog wanders freely and your kids play everywhere.

Tomorrow, someone else's dog shows up unannounced at your campsite... while you're cooking breakfast.

Campground karma has a way of evening things out.

ASK YOURSELF THIS

- Would I be okay if someone else's pet or child did this at my site?
- Am I supervising—or just assuming it's fine?
- Is this behavior respectful of shared space?

If there's doubt, it's usually worth stepping in.

BOTTOM LINE

Campgrounds are meant to be fun for families and pet owners, but that fun works best with a little structure.

When kids and pets know the boundaries, everyone enjoys the campground more. Including you.

CHAPTER FOUR

DOG POOP:

Yes, It Gets Its Own Chapter

Dogs are great. They're loyal, adorable, and one of the best parts of camping for a lot of people.

Dog poop, however, is not.

Somehow, in a place filled with nature, fresh air, and people walking barefoot in flip-flops, dog poop still manages to be the most universally hated campground problem.

And yet...it persists.

How to Accidentally become THAT camper

Your dog does their business near your site, or worse, near someone else's.

You notice. You definitely notice.

But you think:

- "I'll grab it on the way back."
- "No one saw."
- "It's basically in the woods."
- "I don't have a bag right now."

So you leave it.

Later, a fellow camper steps in it. Or a kid rides through it. Or someone smells something suspicious.

And somewhere nearby, you pretend this has nothing to do with you.

Why This Actually Matters

Dog poop isn't just gross, it's inconsiderate and unsanitary.

Campgrounds are shared spaces. People walk, kids play, pets sniff everything, and shoes travel from the ground straight into RVs.

Leaving dog waste behind:

- Ruins shared areas
- Creates health concerns
- Makes campgrounds less welcoming to pet owners overall
- Gives responsible dog owners a bad reputation

No one should have to watch where they step quite *that* carefully on vacation.

What to Do Instead

This one is simple, and thankfully, very fixable.

- Always carry poop bags.
- Pick it up immediately.
- Tie bags securely.
- Dispose of them in designated trash areas.

If your dog tends to go far from your site, bring the bag *with you*. Hoping you'll remember later is how campground legends are born.

Location Matters

Where your dog goes is just as important as whether you clean it up.

- Avoid other campsites.
- Stay out of high-traffic areas.
- Use designated pet walk zones when available.
- Don't let dogs wander off-leash to find their "perfect spot."

Your neighbor's campsite is not your dog's bathroom.

The Poop Bag Situation

Let's address the mysterious phenomenon of bagged poop left on the ground.

If you bag it... you must also *remove it*.

Leaving a neatly tied bag on the ground does not make it less gross. It just adds confusion.

If the plan is "I'll grab it later," please know:

- People don't know that.
- People don't trust that.
- People will remember it.

Take it with you.

Campground Karma

Today, you skip picking up after your dog.

Tomorrow, you step in something that makes you check your shoe in disbelief.

Campground karma is very specific.

Ask Yourself This

- Would I want to step here?
- Would I want my kid playing here?
- Would I want my dog sniffing this?

If the answer is no, grab the bag.

Bottom Line

Dog-friendly campgrounds stay dog-friendly because people do the right thing.

Picking up after your dog is one of the easiest ways to be a great campground neighbor, and one of the fastest ways to avoid becoming *that* camper.

CHAPTER FIVE

LIGHTS:

WHEN YOUR CAMPSITE CAN BE SEEN FROM SPACE

Campgrounds are one of the few places left where darkness is actually part of the experience.

Stars show up. Campfires glow. Headlights pass quietly through the loop.

Which is why nothing kills the vibe faster than a campsite lit up like a 24-hour convenience store.

Lights matter more than people realize, especially after dark.

HOW TO ACCIDENTALLY BECOME THAT CAMPER

You arrive at your site and flip on *all* the lights.

Porch light. Awning lights. Step lights. Interior lights shining through every window. Maybe a string of LEDs set to a color that can be seen from space.

You leave them on while you sit outside. You leave them on when you go inside. You leave them on overnight because... why not?

Across the way, your neighbor's RV is now glowing softly in your reflection. Their bedroom looks like it's noon. They consider buying blackout curtains mid-trip.

Why This Actually Matters

Light pollution doesn't stop at your campsite.

Bright lights:

- Shine directly into neighboring RV windows
- Disrupt sleep
- Ruin night vision and stargazing
- Make it harder to enjoy the campground atmosphere

Many campers come specifically for quiet *and* darkness. Excessive lighting takes that away.

What to Do Instead

You don't need to sit in total darkness. You just need to be intentional.

- Use the minimum lighting needed.
- Choose softer, downward-facing lights.

- Turn off awning and decorative lights when not in use.
- Close blinds if interior lights are bright.

If you're going to bed, lights should follow shortly after.

Motion Lights Are Still Lights

Motion-activated lights can be helpful, but they can also become a surprise strobe show.

If your motion light:

- Activates every time someone walks by
- Flashes directly into other sites
- Turns on repeatedly throughout the night

...it might be doing more harm than good.

Adjust the sensitivity, reposition it, or turn it off overnight.

Late Nights and Early Mornings

Lights matter most when people are sleeping.

- Use headlamps or small flashlights instead of flooding the site.
- Avoid turning on bright exterior lights early in the morning.
- Be mindful when arriving late or leaving early.

The less noticeable you are, the better you're doing.

Campground Karma

Tonight, your lights shine all night long.

Tomorrow, someone else's porch light beams straight into your bedroom window at 3am.

Campground karma never sleeps, and apparently, neither do porch lights.

Ask Yourself This

- Would this light bother me if it were shining into my RV?
- Is this necessary right now?
- Could this be dimmer or turned off?

If you hesitate, adjust the switch.

Bottom Line

Lighting should enhance the campground, not overpower it.

When you respect the darkness, you help everyone sleep better, relax more, and enjoy the experience they came for... stars included.

CHAPTER SIX

CAMPFIRES & COOKING:
SMOKE, SMELLS & UNWRITTEN RULES

Campfires are one of the best parts of camping. They bring people together, slow things down, and make even the simplest meal feel special.

They can also turn a peaceful campground into a smoky, eye-watering situation if a little awareness goes missing.

Campfire and cooking etiquette isn't about taking the fun out of camping. It's about understanding that what feels cozy at your site might feel overwhelming at someone else's.

HOW TO ACCIDENTALLY BECOME THAT CAMPER

You light a fire without checking the wind. Within minutes, the smoke is blowing directly into your neighbor's open windows, their chairs, and possibly their dinner.

You shrug. Smoke happens.

Then dinner starts cooking. The smell drifts. And drifts. And lingers. Someone nearby starts wondering why their campsite smells like burnt bacon mixed with regret. They knew they should have booked site 52 instead.

Meanwhile, you're sitting comfortably in a cloud-free zone, unaware that your neighbor is rotating their chair for the fourth time trying to escape the smoke.

Why This Actually Matters

Smoke doesn't respect campsite boundaries. It moves wherever the wind takes it, and strong or constant smoke can ruin someone's ability to enjoy their space.

Campfires also come with safety concerns. Flying embers, unattended fires, and oversized flames can make neighbors uneasy, even if nothing goes wrong.

What to Do Instead

A few small habits can keep campfires enjoyable for everyone.

- Check wind direction before lighting a fire
- Keep fires small and manageable
- Use dry, appropriate firewood to reduce smoke
- Extinguish the fire fully when you're done

If smoke consistently blows into nearby sites, it's okay to pause, adjust, or even put the fire out. That flexibility goes a long way.

FIRE SAFETY ISN'T OPTIONAL

Every campground has rules about fires for a reason.

- Follow fire bans and local restrictions
- Never leave a fire unattended
- Keep water or a fire extinguisher nearby
- Make sure fires are completely out before leaving or going to bed.

Nothing ends a camping trip faster, or more dramatically, than ignoring fire safety.

SHARED FIRES AND FRIENDLY INVITES

Campfires can be social. But not every fire is an invitation.

Before pulling up a chair at someone else's fire:

- Wait to be invited
- Ask before adding wood
- Respect when people are winding down

And if you do invite others over, great, but don't assume it's an open-door policy for the entire campground.

Campground Karma

Tonight, your smoke drifts into someone else's site.

Tomorrow, the wind shifts, and suddenly your morning coffee tastes like your neighbor's campfire leftovers.

Campground karma loves a good breeze.

Ask Yourself This

- Where is the smoke going right now?
- Would this smell bother me if I were next door?
- Is this fire adding to the campground experience, or taking away from it?

Those answers are usually obvious.

Bottom Line

Campfires and cooking are meant to be enjoyed, not endured.

With a little awareness, you can keep your fire cozy, your food delicious, and your neighbors happy—all without sacrificing the parts of camping that make it special.

CHAPTER SEVEN

VEHICLES & MOVEMENT:

Golf Carts, Bikes, and the Art of Not Being a Hazard

Campgrounds are not parking lots. They're also not racetracks, parade routes, or test tracks for your golf cart's top speed.

They're shared spaces filled with people walking dogs, kids wobbling on bikes, and campers carrying coffee who are absolutely not prepared for sudden chaos.

How vehicles move through a campground matters more than most people realize.

How to Accidentally become THAT camper

You hop on a golf cart and treat the campground loop like it's your personal cruising strip.

You drive just a little faster than necessary. Music playing. Phone in hand. You wave cheerfully as you zip past people walking, assuming everyone sees you coming.

Later, you idle your truck for way too long while loading up. Early morning. Late evening. Doesn't matter, you'll "just be a minute."

Meanwhile, your neighbors are:

- Holding their breath as kids cross the road.
- Wondering why their RV is vibrating.
- Questioning every life choice that put them next to you.

WHY THIS ACTUALLY MATTERS

Campgrounds mix pedestrians, bikes, pets, and vehicles in close quarters. There's very little margin for error.

Fast-moving carts, bikes, or vehicles can:

- Startle kids and animals
- Create real safety risks
- Break the calm, relaxed feel people came for

Idling engines bring noise, fumes, and vibration. These are especially noticeable when people are sleeping or relaxing nearby.

Even when nothing *goes wrong*, it can still make others uncomfortable.

What to Do Instead

Moving through a campground should feel slow, predictable, and boring. That's a good thing.

- Drive well below posted speed limits.
- Yield to pedestrians, bikes, and pets. Always!
- Turn engines off if you'll be stopped more than a moment.

For golf carts and bikes:

- Keep speeds low.
- Watch corners carefully.
- Skip the loud music, especially early and late.
- Assume someone could step out at any moment.

Slow movement keeps everyone safer, and keeps the campground feeling peaceful.

Early Departures and Late Arrivals

Sometimes travel schedules don't line up perfectly. It happens.

But arriving late or leaving early is where extra courtesy matters most.

- Use minimal lighting
- Close doors gently
- Avoid unnecessary engine revving

If it feels like you're sneaking around, you're probably doing it right.

PARKING ISN'T A FREE-FOR-ALL

Campsites are designed for specific vehicles and setups.

- Don't block roads or access points.
- Don't park in empty sites that aren't yours.
- Don't assume unused space is shared space.

Just because a spot *looks* open doesn't mean it's available.

CAMPGROUND KARMA

Today, you speed through the loop and idle forever.

Tomorrow, someone else blocks the road while you're trying to leave, or cruises past your site during nap time.

Campground karma loves a traffic situation.

ASK YOURSELF THIS

- Am I moving slower than I think I need to?
- Could this startle someone nearby?
- Is this trip necessary right now?

If the answer isn't clear, slow it down, or wait.

Bottom Line

The best campground traffic is barely noticeable.

When vehicles, bikes, and carts move calmly and predictably, the campground stays safe, relaxed, and enjoyable for everyone.

CHAPTER EIGHT

SOCIAL ETIQUETTE:

OVERSHARING, BORROWING, AND KNOWING WHEN TO RETREAT

Campgrounds are social by nature. People wave. Small talk happens. Conversations spark over campfires, dogs, or the universal struggle of leveling an RV.

But there's a fine line between being friendly and becoming... a lot.

Good campground social etiquette is about reading the moment. It's about knowing when to engage, and when to politely disappear.

HOW TO ACCIDENTALLY BECOME THAT CAMPER

You see someone sitting outside their RV with a cup of coffee. You assume this means they're available for a full conversation.

You wander over. You sit down without being invited. You share your entire travel history, your medical updates, and a detailed recap of your last campground disagreement.

Your neighbor nods politely, checks their watch, and says, "Well…" several times without success.

You stay.

Why This Actually Matters

Camping is often about downtime. People may be:

- Enjoying quiet moments
- Recharging socially
- Spending time with family
- Working remotely
- Mentally clocked out

Unplanned, long conversations can feel intrusive, even when the intent is friendly.

Borrowing items can be similar. While campers often help each other out, repeatedly asking for supplies or returning items late can create tension.

What to Do Instead

Friendly campground interactions work best when they're light and optional.

- Start with a wave or short greeting.
- Let the other person guide the length of the conversation.
- Watch for cues like short answers, turning away, or packing up.
- Exit gracefully when energy shifts.

A good rule: if someone stands up, starts tidying, or says "Well...," it's time to go.

Borrowing: A Delicate Dance

Campers are generous, but borrowing has unspoken rules.

- Ask once, not repeatedly.
- Return items promptly and clean.
- Don't assume availability.
- Replace consumables if used.

Borrowing should feel helpful, not habitual.

Alcohol and Campground Personalities

Alcohol changes the vibe. Conversations get louder. Stories get longer. Boundaries get looser.

If alcohol is involved:

- Keep volume in check.
- Be extra aware of noise and space.
- Remember not everyone nearby is on the same schedule , or wavelength.

What feels like harmless fun can easily cross into disruption without realizing it.

CAMPGROUND KARMA

Tonight, you trap someone in a conversation they can't escape.

Tomorrow, you're the one nodding politely while someone recounts their entire RV maintenance history.

Campground karma loves a long story.

ASK YOURSELF THIS

- Was I invited or did I invite myself?
- Am I talking more than I'm listening?
- Are they showing signs they want space?

Those answers usually tell you what to do next.

BOTTOM LINE

Being friendly is one of the best parts of camping.

Being *aware* is what makes it enjoyable for everyone.

When in doubt, keep interactions light, kind, and easy to exit. The best campground neighbors know when to say hello and when to head back to their own site.

CHAPTER NINE

DEPARTURE DAY:

PACKING UP WITHOUT WAKING THE ENTIRE CAMPGROUND

Departure day always sneaks up on you.

One minute you're enjoying your last cup of campground coffee, and the next you're staring at the clock, mentally calculating drive time, dump station lines, and how long it's going to take to remember where everything goes.

Leaving a campground doesn't have to be stressful, or loud. But for some reason, departure day is when campground etiquette tends to disappear.

How to Accidentally become THAT camper

It's early. The sun is barely up. Birds are doing their thing.

You start slamming storage doors. The truck idles while you

reorganize the entire backseat. Someone yells directions from across the site. A chair scrapes. A hitch clanks. The engine revs "just to warm it up."

You tell yourself, *We're just getting out of here.*

Meanwhile, your neighbors are awake now. They weren't planning to be, but here we are.

Why This Actually Matters

Departure mornings are when many campers are:

- Sleeping in
- Packing quietly later in the morning
- Enjoying a slow final breakfast
- Trying to savor their last peaceful moments

Sudden, repetitive noise, breaks that calm fast. Even campers who understand early departures still appreciate effort and awareness.

It's not about being silent. It's about being considerate.

What to Do Instead

A little planning makes departure day smoother for everyone.

- Pack non-essential items the night before.
- Close doors and compartments gently.
- Keep conversations low and close to your RV.
- Turn engines on only when you're ready to move.

- Avoid revving or extended idling.

If you're leaving very early, think "stealth mode." Quiet, efficient, and respectful.

The Dump Station Effect

Dump stations are a shared experience, and patience is key.

- Have hoses and supplies ready.
- Move efficiently.
- Clean up after yourself.
- Don't block traffic while reorganizing.

No one wants to start their travel day waiting longer than necessary because someone decided this was the perfect time to sort their storage bins.

Final Walkthroughs Matter

Before you pull out:

- Check for trash.
- Look for forgotten items.
- Make sure the site is clean.

Leaving a campsite better than you found it is one of the simplest ways to be a great campground neighbor, even after you're gone.

Campground Karma

Today, you wake the loop with your early-morning exit.

Tomorrow, someone else fires up their engine right next to you during a well-earned nap.

Campground karma loves a noisy goodbye.

Ask Yourself This

- Am I doing anything louder than it needs to be?
- Could this be done later, or last?
- Would I appreciate this noise if I were still sleeping?

If the answer makes you pause, adjust.

Bottom Line

Departure day doesn't have to feel rushed, chaotic, or disruptive.

With a little preparation and awareness, you can leave the campground quietly, respectfully, and on good terms, without becoming the camper everyone remembers for the wrong reasons.

CHAPTER TEN

THE GOAL:

BE THE CAMPER EVERYONE HOPES PARKS NEXT TO THEM

By now, you've probably recognized a few behaviors.
Maybe in other people.
Maybe, bravely, in yourself.

That's the point.

Campground etiquette isn't about being perfect. It's about being aware. The campers who cause the least friction aren't the ones who follow every rule flawlessly, they're the ones who pay attention to how their choices affect the people around them.

And the good news? That's completely doable.

What the Best Campground Neighbors Have in Common

They don't have the biggest rigs or the flashiest setups.
They aren't trying to camp better than anyone else.
They're just mindful of the people around them.

They're considerate.

Great campground neighbors tend to:

- Keep noise, lights, and movement in check
- Respect space and boundaries
- Pick up after their pets
- Supervise kids without killing the fun
- Read the room socially
- Leave sites clean and calm

They understand that camping is a shared experience, and they act like it.

Awareness Beats Rules Every Time

You can memorize campground rules and still miss the point.

Awareness is what actually keeps the peace:

- Noticing when sound carries
- Watching where light spills
- Seeing when someone wants space
- Adjusting without being asked

Most campground conflicts don't come from bad intentions.

They come from people being wrapped up in their own trip and forgetting that others are sharing the same space.

A small adjustment can completely change someone else's experience.

You Don't Have to Lose the Fun

This part matters.

Being a good campground neighbor does *not* mean:

- Sitting in silence
- Turning off all joy
- Keeping kids or pets miserable
- Stressing over every little thing

It just means enjoying your trip without turning it into someone else's problem.

Laugh. Cook. Hang out. Relax.
Just do it with a little situational awareness.

When in Doubt, Use the Camper Test

If you're unsure about something, ask yourself:

- Would this bother me if it were happening next door?
- Would I want this at 6am? At 10pm?
- Is this necessary, or just convenient for me?

Those questions solve most campground etiquette dilemmas instantly.

Campground Karma (One Last Time)

The way you camp affects the way others experience their trip.

When you're considerate, flexible, and aware, that energy tends to come back around, sometimes immediately, sometimes later.

Campground karma favors the campers who make things easier, calmer, and more enjoyable for everyone.

Bottom Line

You don't have to be perfect to be a great campground neighbor.

You just have to care a little.

And if you're reading this book, laughing, nodding, and thinking about how to make your next trip smoother, you're already well on your way to being the camper everyone hopes parks next to them.

FINAL NOTE

If you're reading this, chances are you already care about being a good campground neighbor, and that puts you ahead of the game.

Campground etiquette isn't about perfection or following every rule to the letter. It's about awareness. About remembering that campgrounds are shared spaces, and small choices can make a big difference for the people around you.

If this book helped you laugh, recognize a habit or two, or make even one small adjustment on your next trip, then it's done exactly what it was meant to do.

Here's to peaceful campgrounds, shared spaces, and being the camper everyone hopes parks next to them.

ABOUT THE AUTHOR

Erin Graves is an RV camper who loves good campground neighbors, peaceful mornings, and camping experiences that feel enjoyable for everyone involved. She has spent years camping with her two favorite camping companions, her husband and son. On those camping trips, she has observed what makes trips work well, and she's learned that awareness goes a long way.

She shares RV life, outdoor cooking, and travel content through **Campin' Erin**, where she connects with a community of campers who appreciate humor, practicality, and shared love for the campground.

CAMPIN ERIN
"HEY CAMPERS!"

www.ingramcontent.com/pod-product-compliance
Lightning Source LLC
Chambersburg PA
CBHW060202070426
42447CB00033B/2292